Skills for Young Writers

Written by

Kris Robinson-Cobb

Theresa Gerig

Glenda Sible Shull

Inside Illustrations
by
Pat Biggs

Cover Illustration
by
Vickie Lane

Publishers
Instructional Fair • TS Denison
Grand Rapids, Michigan 49544

Permission to Reproduce

Instructional Fair • TS Denison grants the right to the individual purchaser to reproduce the student activity materials in this book for non-commercial individual or classroom use only. Reproduction for an entire school or school system is strictly prohibited. No part of this publication may be reproduced for storage in a retrieval system, or transmitted in any form or by any means, electronic, mechanical, recording, or otherwise, without the prior written permission of the publisher. For information regarding permission write to: Instructional Fair • TS Denison, P.O. Box 1650, Grand Rapids, MI 49501.

Credits

Authors: Kris Robinson-Cobb, Theresa Gerig, Glenda Sible Shull
Cover Artist: Vickie Lane
Illustrations: Pat Biggs
Project Director: Rhonda DeWaard
Editors: Elizabeth Flikkema, Sharon Kirkwood, Rhonda DeWaard
Production/Layout: Pat Geasler

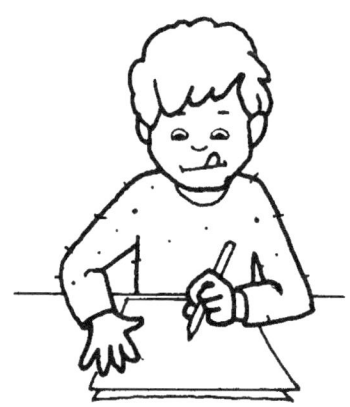

Standard Book Number: 1-56822-583-0
Skills for Young Writers–2
Copyright © 1997 by Instructional Fair • TS Denison
2400 Turner Avenue NW
Grand Rapids, Michigan 49544

All Rights Reserved • Printed in the USA

Table of Contents

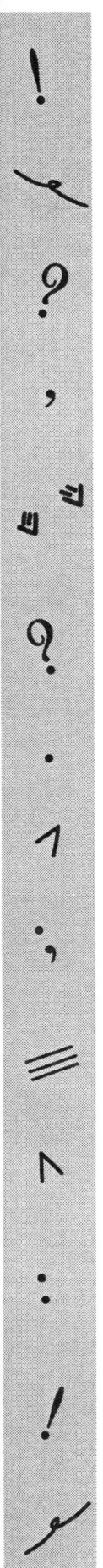

Introduction/About the Authors 4
Steps for Successful Writing 5
Proofreading Symbols/Teacher Tips for Editing 6
Teacher Tips for Encouraging Young Writers 7
My Family (complete sentences, spelling) 8
Leaves (series commas, sequence clue words) 9
Saturday (capital letters, plurals) 10
Who Am I? (complete sentences, punctuation, spelling) 11
Ben's Turtle (abbreviations, capitals for days of week, sentences
    that don't belong) 12
Tony (punctuation, past-tense verbs) 13
Dear Mr. Storekeeper (articles, friendly letter format) 14
Skating (contractions; *wanta, gonna, dontcha*) 15
Ducks (capital letters, series commas) 16
Mom (series commas, complete sentences) 17
A Boxing Turtle? (contractions, sentences that don't belong) 18
Terry's Fun Day (punctuation, capital letters, homophones) 19
Fish School (contractions, spelling) 20
Sunflower (run-on sentences, paragraph indentation) 21
Grandma and Me (contractions, unnecessary apostrophes,
    paragraph indentation) 22
Zoo (verbs, pronouns in the subject) 23
Dear Baby Sister (friendly letter format, homophones) 24
Bear Cubs (series commas, homophones) 25
Stars (punctuation, paragraph indentation, capital letters) 26
A Princess's Wish (plurals, punctuation) 27
If I Had a Baby Sister . . . (complete sentences, contractions) 28
Rainy Day (verbs, contractions) 29
Dear Grandma and Grandpa (punctuation, capital letters, friendly letter
    format) 30
A Fish Tale (punctuation, *a* and *an*) 31
What If . . . (underline titles, capital letters) 32
Seasons (capitals for months, series commas) 33
Thunder Storm (punctuation, capital letters) 34
Transportation (abbreviations, possessives) 35
Spring (run-on sentences, series commas) 36
Starfish (verbs, plurals) 37
The Tree House (*wanna, gonna, dontcha*; quotation marks) 38–39
Soaring (quotation marks, sequence clue words) 40–41
Hobbies (pronouns in the subject, changing *y* to *i* for plurals, sequence
    clue words) 42
Answer Keys 43-48

Introduction

Skills for Young Writers is a reproducible book designed to turn novice writers into fluent writers. These high-interest grade-appropriate lessons can be used to enhance and strengthen proofreading and revising skills.

This book contains fiction and nonfiction selections which focus on various skills such as grammar, punctuation, and spelling. Suggested Revisions/Extensions at the end of each lesson provide additional activities that may be considered for expanding writing skills.

The lessons are designed to be used as teaching transparencies and student worksheets. There is ample space on each page to allow for corrections. In some cases, revisions or extensions may require a separate sheet of paper. The Answer Keys at the back of the book may be used as a guide for the teacher, although students may include additional revisions. Skills taught in these lessons may be reinforced in students' personal writing.

About the Authors

Kris Robinson-Cobb is currently a second grade teacher in St. Joe, Indiana. She received her BA and MA degrees in Education from Indiana University. She has taught in the elementary grades for 17 years.

Theresa Gerig has taught 20 years in the elementary school setting. She received her BA and Masters in Education from Indiana University. She lives near Ft. Wayne, Indiana, and is presently teaching third grade.

Glenda Sible Shull is a graduate of Manchester College and Indiana University. She is an author and an elementary teacher.

Steps for Successful Writing

Prewriting

- Brainstorm topics you might like to write about.
- Create a list of things you could write about each topic.
- Choose the topic you know the most about and that would be of interest to others.
- Collect information.
- Consider your audience and purpose for writing.

Writing

- Write a rough draft focusing on what you want to say rather than the spelling and mechanics.
- Skip every other line when writing your rough draft to leave space for corrections.

Revising

- Read your draft, making changes for interest and clarity.
- Ask another person to listen to your writing and to offer suggestions for improvement.

Editing and Proofreading

- Proofread your writing for spelling, punctuation, and grammar errors.
- Read your piece to an adult.
- Correct and neatly recopy or type your final draft.
- Choose an attention-grabbing title.

Proofreading Symbols

≡	capital letter	Max smith ...
/	lower-case letter	We like to Ĕat ...
⊙	add period	It was fun⊙
?	add question mark	Do you like pizza?
∧	insert, add this	Ten^people were coming ...
ℯ	delete, take out	Jump all around ...
⋎	add apostrophe	The bike was Sarah's.
♨ ♩	add quotation marks	Jonathon yelled, Supper!
⌐	indent	⌐The boy ...

Teacher Tips for Editing

- Students may gain more understanding if some selections are corrected with the class as a group before requiring students to make corrections independently.

- If using a transparency, use brightly colored markers for clarity.

- Count skill mistakes and give this number to the students to motivate and guide them.

- When using selections for individual work, allow students to edit and revise in colored pencil or pen.

Teacher Tips for Encouraging Young Writers

- Provide students with several ideas and options for their writing.

- Encourage students to write their rough drafts without concern about spelling. Corrections in spelling will come during proofreading.

- Have students share their rough drafts with a buddy or a small group to get suggestions for revisions.

- Provide red pencils or colored pens for children to use while proofreading for spelling and grammar errors.

- Hold individual conferences to read and discuss written work.

- If students have written the rough copy, allow them to type the final draft if possible.

- Encourage children to illustrate their stories. Very young children may want to illustrate before they write, while others will be ready to write before illustrating.

- Children love to share their final products. Staple stories and illustrations into a book and let children read to other students or classrooms.

- Publish stories in a class book to be shared in your reading area. You may want to place a copy in the school library.

- Maintain individual portfolios, including samples of student work.

Name _____

✎ Skill Lessons
1. Use complete sentences.
2. Correct the misspelled words.

My Family

I have a very lrge family. I liv with my mom and dad. Three bruthers and two sisters. In a bigg house. and a bigg yrd. We hav lots of fun togethr.

Suggested Revisions
- Include more details about the family members.
- Tell some things the family does for fun.

✏️ Skill Lessons

1. Use commas in a series.
2. Use the words *first,* *then,* and *finally* to make the story sequence clear.

Leaves

I like to watch the leaves change in the fall. They turn red yellow and brown. They become dry and crunchy. My friends and I make big piles of leaves jump in them and roll in them. Somebody rakes the leaves.

Suggested Revision

- Continue the story. Tell more about leaves.

Skill Lessons
1. Use capital letters correctly.
2. Add -s or -es to make the underlined words plural.

Saturday

on saturday, i will see <u>witch</u> in black <u>dress</u>. i'll see <u>pirate</u> with black <u>patch</u>. on saturday, carved <u>pumpkin</u> will be glowing next to <u>bush</u>. saturday is halloween.

Suggested Revisions
- Tell about other things you see on Halloween.
- Add descriptive words.

Skill Lessons

1. Use complete sentences.
2. Place a punctuation mark at the end of each sentence.
3. Correct the misspelled words.

Who Am I?

I wear blak clothes. I have a pointy hat. A blak dress with blak shoes. A broom. I have a wart at the end of my pointy nos. Long, red fingernails. When I say, "Trick or treat," I will laugh a scary laugh Who am I

Suggested Revisions

- Add descriptive words.
- Add a sentence describing the character's voice.

Name _____

✎ Skill Lessons
1. Write the abbreviations correctly.
2. Use capital letters for the days of the week.
3. Cross out the sentence that doesn't belong.

Ben's Turtle

On monday, Ben found a turtle in the pond. It was raining. On tuesday, he gave it to mrs Flora. On wednesday, mrs Flora took the turtle to school. Her second-grade class watched the turtle on thursday. On friday, mrs Flora returned the turtle to Ben. On saturday, he let it go in the same pond.

Suggested Revision
- Add a sentence describing the turtle.

Skill Lessons

1. Place a punctuation mark at the end of each sentence.
2. Write the correct action word.

Tony

Tony standed at home plate The first ball gone by, and the umpire called, "Ball one!" Tony swinged the bat at the next ball, but he missed He tightened his grip on the bat and watch the pitcher throw the ball. Tony shutted his eyes as he swinged the bat He heard a loud "smack!"

Suggested Revisions

- Continue the story. What happened next?
- Add details about the setting.
- Write an interesting title for the story.

Skill Lessons
1. Use the words *a, an,* and *the* correctly.
2. Add punctuation and capital letters to this friendly letter.

Dear Mr. Storekeeper

october 21 1998

dear Mr. Storekeeper

I am building a underwater house. I would like to order some supplies to help with the project.

I need an sawfish to cut an wood, an hammerhead shark to pound an nails, and an boxfish to hold my tools.

Here is an sand dollar as payment.

sincerely

Mr. Buzz Saw

Suggested Revisions
- Give the storekeeper a name.
- Add other supplies to the list.

Name _____

✏️ Skill Lessons
1. Write contractions correctly.
2. Use the correct spelling to replace the words *wanta*, *gonna*, and *dontcha*.

Skating

Today our class is gonna go skating. Were gonna have fun.

I will skate with my friends and my teacher. Therell be games like "Hokey Pokey" and "Limbo." The winners of the games are gonna receive prizes.

If my friends and I get hot, well buy a cold drink at the snack bar.

Dontcha wanta go too?

Suggested Revision
• Describe other fun activities at the skating party.

Name _____

✎ **Skill Lessons**
1. Use capital letters correctly.
2. Use commas in a series.

Ducks

ducks can swim walk or fly. they do not get cold in the water. oil on their feathers helps keep ducks dry. ducks hatch from eggs. young ducks are called ducklings. the female duck is called a duck. the male duck is called a drake. you can find ducks near ponds lakes rivers and marshes.

Suggested Revision
- Tell about different kinds of ducks.

✏️ Skill Lessons
1. Use commas in a series.
2. Use complete sentences.

Mom

My mom is always very busy. She cooks the food washes the clothes and cleans the house. She feeds the dog pays the bills and sweeps the walk.

Mom is never too busy to help me. She takes care of me. When I am sick. She helps me with my homework. Takes me places. I think my mom is great!

Suggested Revisions
- Give the story an interesting title.
- Include more details about what Mom does.

Name _____

✏️ Skill Lessons
1. Write the contractions correctly.
2. Cross out the sentences that do not belong.

A Boxing Turtle?

How do turtles get their names? A box turtle cant box. Some turtles have soft shells. Map turtles arent able to draw maps. Painted turtles cant paint pictures. Some turtles eat flies.

Suggested Revisions
- Add one more thing that a turtle can't do.
- Add an interesting ending to complete the story.

Skill Lessons

1. Place a punctuation mark at the end of each sentence.
2. Use capital letters correctly.
3. Use the correct homophones.

Terry's Fun Day

Terry watched three playful monkeys they were swinging on a blew swing he saw won lazy bare the bear was sleeping in a whole Terry fed for elephants they took peanuts from him with their trunks Terry watched won bird fly hi in the sky Terry laughed at the seals they played with a ball in the water Terry did knot want to go home

Suggested Revisions

- Write a sentence at the beginning telling where Terry is.
- Combine two short sentences to form a long sentence.

Skill Lessons
1. Write the contractions correctly.
2. Correct the misspelled words.

Fish School

Little fish, come bite my hook.

Im in need of somthing to cook.

Into the frying pane you will goe.

Itll be hot, you may not know.

Im licking my lipes because youll taste great.

Hurry up fish, its getting late!

Right by my line the fish all pass.

You see theyre in a special class.

The fish are swimming where its cool.

Theyre learning to be safe in schol.

Suggested Revision
- Add one rhyming couplet to the poem.

Name _____

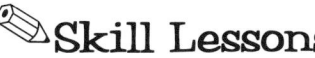 Skill Lessons
1. Correct the run-on sentences.
2. Indent the first line of the story.

Sunflower

If I could be a plant, I would be a sunflower. I want to be a sunflower because sunflowers are tall. Their bright heads decorate fields and gardens and people eat sunflower seeds. Oil from the seeds can be used for cooking birds and squirrels like to eat sunflower seeds. Most of all, I would like to be a sunflower because yellow is my favorite color.

Suggested Revisions
- Add descriptive words.
- Give the story an interesting title.

Name _____

✎ **Skill Lessons**
1. Write the contractions correctly.
2. Remove unnecessary apostrophes.
3. Indent the first line in the story.

Grandma and Me

Its fun to be with just my grandma. She takes me fishing, but doesnt make me bait the hook. Then she lets me make my own sandwich, and I dont have to eat the crust's. Then we walk to the park and stay as long as we want. Then I help her bake cookie's and eat half of the dough. We have fun together, just Grandma and me.

Suggested Revisions
- Give the story an interesting title.
- Begin sentences with words other than *then*.

Name _____

✎ Skill Lessons
1. Write the correct action words.
2. Name yourself last in the subject.

Zoo

I and my dad goed to the zoo. The monkeys liked my dad's bright red hat. One monkey reached through the bars of the cage and tooked the hat. The monkey throwed it in a tree. A fast, brown monkey climbs up the tree and throwed the hat out of the cage. A parrot flied down to pick up the hat. I and my dad watched the parrot flied to a tree, and then the parrot watch us.

Suggested Revisions
- Continue the story. What happened next?
- Add descriptive words.

Skill Lessons

1. Add punctuation and capital letters.
2. Use the correct homophones.

Dear Baby Sister

May 12 1999

Dear baby sister

    I am so happy that you are coming two live with us. I can't wait to meat you. I no that their are many things that will be knew to you. I will teach you what I no.

    I will teach you how to roller-skate. Put the skates on you're feet and tie the laces. Stand up. Move you're feet. Soon you will no how to roll write along with me.

your loving sister

Jenny

Suggested Revisions

- Add the words *first, then,* and *finally* to the skating directions.
- Write about other things you will teach your baby sister.

Name _____

✎ Skill Lessons
1. Use commas in a series.
2. Use the correct homophones.

Bear Cubs

Bare cubs are born during the winter. Usually to cubs are born at one time. When they are born, they have know fur and they can't sea. At first they just eat sleep and stay near their mother. In the spring, the mother bare brings the cubs out of the den. They walk run and play together. The forest is full of interesting things four the cubs to sea smell and taste.

Suggested Revisions
- Tell about different kinds of bears.
- Add a sentence to end the article.

Name _____

✏️ Skill Lessons
1. Place a punctuation mark at the end of each sentence.
2. Indent the first line of the article.
3. Use capital letters correctly.

Stars

Did you know that even on a sunny day the stars are in the sky stars are always in the sky you can't see the stars in the daytime because the sun's light is so bright our sun is a star it is the star nearest to the earth all stars shine with their own light they are very hot stars seem to twinkle because the light comes to us through moving air

Suggested Revisions
- Combine two short sentences to form a long sentence.
- Give the article an interesting title.

Name _____

✎ Skill Lessons
1. Add -s or -es to make the underlined words plural.
2. Place a punctuation mark at the end of each sentence.

A Princess's Wish

The twins had <u>box</u> filled with magic building <u>block</u> One day they built two <u>castle</u> In one castle, there lived a princess In the other castle, there lived three wicked <u>witch</u> One day, a bird gave the princess a pretty flower Inside the flower was a fairy that would give the princess three <u>wish</u>

Suggested Revisions
- Write what the princess wished for.
- Add descriptive words.

Name _____

✏️ Skill Lessons
1. Use complete sentences.
2. Write the contractions correctly.

If I Had a Baby Sister

If I had a baby sister, I would buy her toys. We would play together. At the park. Wed swing on the swing set. Slide down the slide. I would pull her in my wagon. Because shed like that. Id like having a baby sister. Would be fun.

Suggested Revisions
- Add descriptive words.
- Include more sentences telling why you'd like to have a baby sister.

✏️ **Skill Lessons**
1. Write the correct action words.
2. Write the contractions correctly.

Rainy Day

It was raining. Theresa couldnt go out to play. She want to read her new book, but she couldnt find the book in her messy room. "There is too many things out of place," Theresa moaned. As she searched, Theresa pick up all of her toys and games and put them on the bed. Finally, she find her book under some stuffed animals.

Theresa look at her bed where she want to read her book. She couldnt find a place to sit on the bed.

Suggested Revisions
- Write an ending to the story.
- Give the story an interesting title.

Skill Lessons

1. Use capital letters correctly.
2. Add punctuation.
3. Add the date to the letter.

Dear Grandma and Grandpa

dear grandma and grandpa

    I had a great time visiting you in florida! I liked swimming in the atlantic ocean and jumping in the waves. the shells we found along the beach in daytona were great for my collection. I really liked seeing the dolphins jumping in the water and the pelicans flying overhead. best of all, I liked going to walt disney world! Thanks for a great vacation!

love

jonathan

Suggested Revision

- Tell what you liked about a real or imaginary visit to Walt Disney World.

Skill Lessons

1. Place the correct punctuation mark at the end of each sentence.
2. Use the words *a* and *an* correctly.

A Fish Tale

The next time you take out your pole and fill an can with worms to go fishing, think about these questions?

Did you ever hear an dogfish bark. Do angelfish fly. Does an goatfish give milk. Does an catfish drink that milk. Can an parrotfish talk. Can an toadfish hop. Does an butterfly fish like flowers. Can you keep things in an boxfish.

Suggested Revisions
- Write an ending to the article.
- Write an interesting title.

Skill Lessons
1. Underline the book titles.
2. Use capital letters correctly.

What If . . .

What if that little girl really wore blue?

Would little blue riding hood be read to you?

Or what if big Clifford turned out to be small?

Would you enjoy clifford, the miniature dog?

What if the dwarfs were really quite tall?

snow white and the seven giants might frighten us all.

Last, but not least, is green eggs and ham.

I'm glad they weren't pancakes. Really I am!

Suggested Revision
- Choose other book titles to change. Add rhyming couplets to the poem.

✏️ Skill Lessons
1. Use capital letters for the months.
2. Use commas in a series.

Seasons

I think of colorful trees and the smell of burning leaves in september october and november. These are the gentle months of fall. In the cold, snowy days of december january and february, I wear a warm coat boots and mittens each day. These are the chilly months of winter. Breezes blow rain falls flowers bloom and birds begin to sing in march april and may. These are the exciting months of spring. In june july and august, I play ball go to the park and run through sprinklers. These are the playful months of summer.

Suggested Revisions
- Write a topic sentence for the article.
- Divide the article into paragraphs and add more details about each season.

Name

✎ Skill Lessons
1. Place a punctuation mark at the end of each sentence.
2. Use capital letters correctly.

Thunder Storm

i lay awake in the quiet house watching the sky grow darker suddenly, there was a bright flash of light there was a loud "crack" the rain began to splash against my window I could see the wind bend the tree branches outside I wanted to hide under my covers, but I knew what I had to do trembling, i slipped quickly out of bed i ran down the hall to the closed door at the end as I hurried inside, i heard the storm roaring outside I jumped in the bed I quickly covered us both with the blanket I snuggled closer to my sleeping brother so he wouldn't be afraid.

Suggested Revisions
- Combine short sentences to form longer sentences.
- Change some sentences so fewer sentences begin with *I*.

Name _____

✎ Skill Lessons
1. Write the abbreviations correctly.
2. Write the possessive nouns correctly.

Transportation

One day, mr and mrs Mouse wanted to visit dr Mole. Mrs Mouses car would not start, so mr and mrs Mouse jumped on their bicycles. Mrs Mouses bicycle had a flat tire. mrs Mouse called mr Rats Taxi Service, but Mr Rats taxi was out of gas.

"We will have to walk," mr Mouse said sadly. "It is a long way."

"I have an idea!" cried mrs Mouse. "Let's take dr Moles subway. He has dug many tunnels straight to his office."

Suggested Revisions
- Give the story an interesting title.
- Write an ending to the story.

Name _____

✏️ Skill Lessons
1. Correct the run-on sentences.
2. Use commas in a series.

Spring

When Joe woke up, the sun was shining in his window and he smiled. It would be a fine day to plant his garden he quickly got up and got out his tractor.

The sun was shining brightly as Joe planted carrots beans corn and beets he covered the seeds with the warm soil and patted it gently, as if tucking the seeds in bed. Then Joe planted the tomato plants cabbage and some turnips and just as he finished, the sun went away and it began to rain.

Joe smiled the warm sunshine the good soil and the gentle rain would make his garden grow.

Suggested Revisions
- Rewrite the story as if you were Joe.
- Give the story an interesting title.

✏️ Skill Lessons
1. Write the correct action words.
2. Form plurals correctly.

Starfish

Starfish are not really fish. They live in the ocean. Most starfish has five armes and can grow a new arm if they lose one. The underside of each arm is covered by tube foots that help the starfish crawl and get food. The starfish has an eyespot on the tip of each arm that can sense light.

Starfish likes to eat mussels, clames, and oysters. To eat, the starfish pushing its stomach out of its mouth. The stomach surrounded the food.

Most starfish lives three to five yeares, but some may live longer.

Suggested Revisions
- Write a concluding sentence about starfish.
- Add an opinion to the article.
- Add an interesting title.

Skill Lessons

1. Write the correct words to replace *wanna, gonna,* and *dontcha.*
2. Add quotation marks correctly.

The Tree House

Do you wanna play ball? asked Ben.

No, said Barry.

Why not? asked Ben.

I wanna go to the tree house, answered Barry.

So the two boys hiked through the tall grass until they came to Barry's tree house.

We're gonna have fun! cried Barry. Ben didn't say anything. What's wrong? asked Barry.

Ben said sadly, I wanna play. Your tree house looks great, but …

Continued on page 39.

The Tree House (Cont.)

But what? asked Barry.

I can't climb that rope, so I can't get in, said Ben.

Dontcha worry, Ben. Just follow me, said Barry. He led Ben to the back of the tree where the branches were low and easy to climb.

We're gonna have fun! yelled Ben.

Suggested Revisions
- Continue the story. Tell what happened next.
- Replace said and asked with other words.

Name _____

✎ Skill Lessons
1. Add quotation marks correctly.
2. Use the words *first, then, next,* and *finally* to make the story sequence clear.

Soaring

A boy and his father ran across the beach watching Red Kite climb high into the sky. Red Kite was now flying. He wanted to explore. He headed for a bird's nest.

Go home, said the bird in the nest.

Not yet, said Red Kite. He raced to a telephone pole.

Go home, said the telephone pole.

Not yet, I want to fly higher, said Red Kite. He soared toward an airplane.

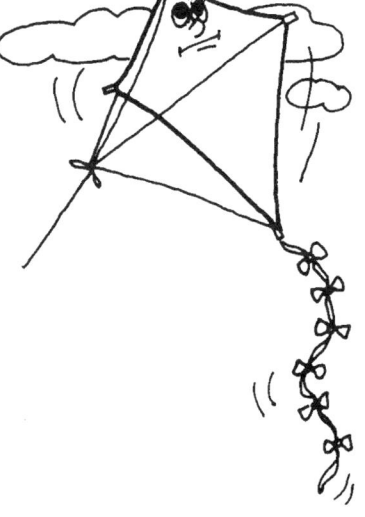

Go home, said the airplane.

Not yet, said Red Kite.

Continued on page 41.

Soaring *(Cont.)*

Come down, said the boy.

Not yet, said Red Kite, jerking on the string.

Come down, said the boy as he pulled harder. Father slowly wound the kite string around the spool.

I'll come down, said Red Kite as he flew to the ground.

Suggested Revisions
- Replace *said* with different words.
- Give the story an interesting title.

Name _____

✏ Skill Lessons
1. Use the pronoun *I* rather than *me* in *the subject*.
2. Spell plurals correctly.
3. Use the words *first, then, next,* and *finally* in the first paragraph.

Hobbies

Steve and me have two favorite hobbys. One hobby is catching butterflys. Steve waits for the butterflys to land on the daisys and the flower bushes. He passes the net to me, and I scoop up the butterflys. Steve and me gently place them in a special insect box. We look through a magnifying glass to observe the butterflys.

The other hobby Steve and me have is finding cloud pictures. Some clouds look like trees with cherrys on them. Other clouds look like ponys pulling buggys.

Steve and me have fun together. Do you have hobbys that you share with a friend?

Suggested Revisions
- Join two sentences with a comma and the word *and*.
- Write an interesting title.

Answer Key

My Family

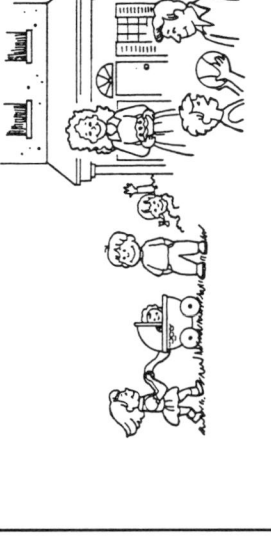

I have a very ~~litle~~ large family. I ~~liv~~ live with my mom and dad. ~~t~~ I have Three ~~bruders~~ brothers and two sisters, ~~in~~ with a ~~bigg~~ big house, ~~and~~ and a ~~big yard~~. We ~~hav~~ have lots of fun ~~togather~~ together.

Page 8

Leaves

I like to watch the leaves change in the fall. First, They turn red, yellow, and brown. Then, They become dry and crunchy. My friends and I make big piles of leaves, jump in them, and roll in them. Finally, Somebody rakes the leaves.

Page 9

Saturday

On saturday, i will see witch(es) in black dress(es). i'll see pirate(s) with black patch(es). On saturday, carved pumpkin(s) will be glowing next to bush(es). saturday is halloween.

Page 10

Who Am I?

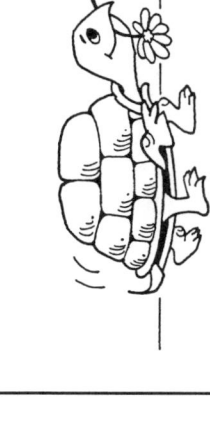

I wear black clothes. I have a pointy hat and a black ~~A black~~. dress with black shoes. I carry a broom. I have a wart at the end of my pointy nose. I have Long, red fingernails. When I say, "Trick or treat," I will laugh a scary laugh. Who am I?

Page 11

Ben's Turtle

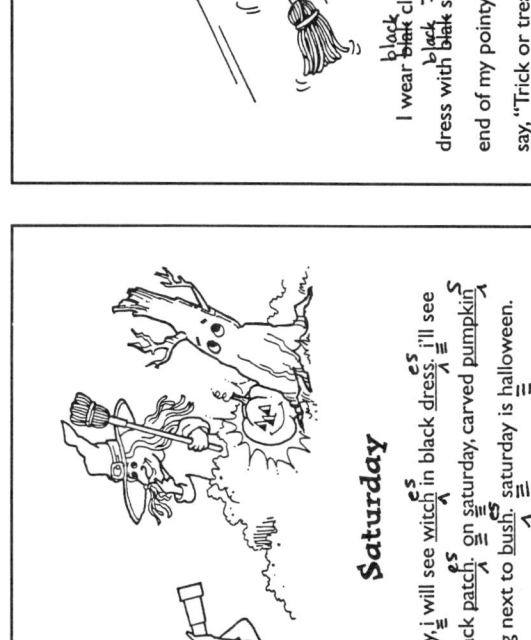

On Monday, Ben found a turtle in the pond. ~~It was raining~~. On Tuesday, he gave it to ~~mrs~~ Mrs. Flora. On Wednesday, ~~mrs~~ Mrs. Flora took the turtle to school. Her second-grade class watched the turtle on Thursday. On Friday, ~~mrs~~ Mrs. Flora returned the turtle to Ben. On Saturday, he let it go in the same pond.

Page 12

Tony

Tony ~~standed~~ stood at home plate. The first ball ~~gone~~ went by, and the umpire called, "Ball one!" Tony ~~swinged~~ swung the bat at the next ball, but he missed. He tightened his grip on the bat and ~~watch~~ watched the pitcher throw the ball. Tony ~~shutted~~ shut his eyes as he ~~swinged~~ swung the bat. He heard a loud "smack!"

Dear Mr. Storekeeper

october 21, 1998

dear Mr. Storekeeper,

I am building ~~a~~ an underwater house. I would like to order some supplies to help with the project.

I need ~~a~~ an sawfish to cut the wood, ~~an~~ a hammerhead shark to pound ~~an~~ the nails, and ~~an~~ a boxfish to hold my tools.

Here is ~~an~~ a sand dollar as payment.

sincerely,

Mr. Buzz Saw

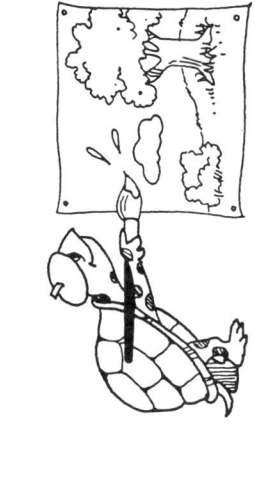

Skating

Today our class is ~~gonna~~ going to go skating. ~~We're gonna~~ We're going to have fun.

I will skate with my friends and my teacher.

There'll be games like "Hokey Pokey" and "Limbo." The winners of the games are ~~gonna~~ going to receive prizes.

If my friends and I get hot, we'll buy a cold drink at the snack bar.

~~Don't cha~~ Don't you want to ~~wanna~~ go too?

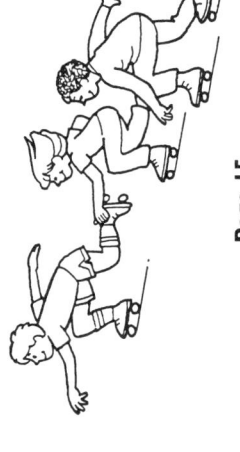

Ducks

ducks can swim, walk, or fly. they do not get cold in the water. oil on their feathers helps keep ducks dry. ducks hatch from eggs. young ducks are called ducklings. the female duck is called a duck. the male duck is called a drake. you can find ducks near ponds, lakes, rivers, and marshes.

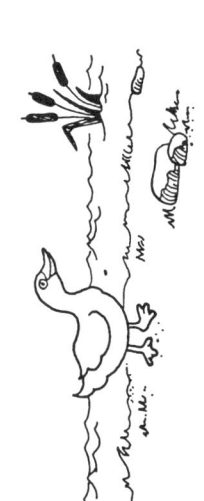

Mom

My mom is always very busy. She cooks the food, washes the clothes, and cleans the house. She feeds the dog, pays the bills, and sweeps the walk.

Mom is never too busy to help me. She takes care of me. When I am sick. She helps me with my homework, and takes me places. I think my mom is great!

A Boxing Turtle?

How do turtles get their names? A box turtle can't box. ~~Some turtles have soft shells.~~ Map turtles aren't able to draw maps. Painted turtles can't paint pictures. ~~Some turtles eat flies.~~

Terry's Fun Day

Terry watched three playful monkeys~~,~~ ^they were swinging on a ~~blew~~ blue swing^he saw ~~was~~ one lazy ~~beer~~ bear^the bear was sleeping in a ~~whole~~ hole. Terry fed ~~foe~~ four elephants^ they took peanuts from him with their trunks^Terry watched ~~won~~ one bird fly ~~hi~~ high in the sky^Terry laughed at the seals^they played with a ball in the water^Terry did not ~~knot~~ want to go home^.

Page 19

Fish School

Little fish, come bite my hook.
I'm in need of ~~something~~ something to cook.
Into the frying ~~pane~~ pan you will ~~gee~~ go.
It'll be hot, you may not know.
I'm licking my ~~lipes~~ lips because you'll taste great.
Hurry up fish, it's getting late!
Right by my line the fish all pass.
You see they're in a special class.
The fish are swimming where it's cool.
They're learning to be safe in ~~school~~ school.

Page 20

Sunflower

If I could be a plant, I would be a sunflower. I want to be a sunflower because sunflowers are tall. Their bright heads decorate fields and gardens^and people eat sunflower seeds. Oil from the seeds can be used for cooking^birds and squirrels like to eat sunflower seeds. Most of all, I would like to be a sunflower because yellow is my favorite color.

Page 21

Grandma and Me

It's fun to be with just my grandma. She takes me fishing, but doesn't make me bait the hook. Then she lets me make my own sandwich, and I don't have to eat the crusts. Then we walk to the park and stay as long as we want. Then I help her bake cookies and eat half of the dough. We have fun together, just Grandma and me.

Page 22

Zoo

My dad and I went ~~and my dad and~~ to the zoo. The monkeys liked my dad's bright red hat. One monkey reached through the bars of the cage and ~~tooked~~ took the hat. The monkey ~~throwed~~ threw it in a tree. A fast, brown monkey ~~climbs~~ climbed up the tree and ~~throwed~~ threw the hat out of the cage. A parrot ~~flied~~ flew down to pick up the hat. ~~and my dad~~ My dad and I watched the parrot ~~flied~~ fly to a tree, and then the parrot ~~watch~~ watched us.

Page 23

Dear Baby Sister

May 12, 1999

Dear baby sister,

I am so happy that you are coming ~~two~~ to live with us. I can't wait to ~~meet~~ meet you. I ~~no~~ know that ~~their~~ there are many things that will be new to you. I will teach you what I ~~no~~ know.

I will teach you how to roller-skate. Put the skates on ~~youre~~ your feet and tie the laces. Stand up. Move ~~youre~~ your feet. Soon you will ~~no~~ know how to roll ~~white~~ right along with me.

Your loving sister,
Jenny

Page 24

Bear Cubs

~~Bare~~ Bear cubs are born during the winter. Usually ~~two~~ cubs are born at one time. When they are born, they have ~~know~~ no fur and they can't ~~feel~~ see. At first they just eat, sleep, and stay near their mother. In the spring, the mother ~~bare~~ bear brings the cubs out of the den. They walk, run, and play together. The forest is full of interesting things ~~four~~ for the cubs to ~~sea~~ see, smell, and taste.

Page 25

Stars

Did you know that even on a sunny day the stars are in the sky? stars are always in the sky, you can't see the stars in the daytime because the sun's light is so bright. Our sun is a star, it is the star nearest to the earth, all stars shine with their own light, they are very hot, stars seem to twinkle because the light comes to us through moving air.

Page 26

A Princess's Wish

The twins had box~~es~~ filled with magic building blocks. In one castle, there lived a princess. In the other castle, there lived three wicked witch~~es~~. One day, a bird gave the princess a pretty flower. Inside the flower was a fairy that would give the princess three wishes.

Page 27

If I Had a Baby Sister

If I had a baby sister, I would buy her toys. We would play together/ ~~A~~ at the park. We'd swing on the swing set, slide down the slide. I would pull her in my wagon because she'd like that. I'd like having a baby sister. It would be fun.

Page 28

Rainy Day

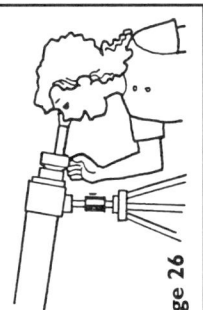

It was raining. Theresa couldn't go out to play. She *wanted* ~~want~~ to read her new book, but she couldn't find the book in her messy room. "There ~~is~~ are too many things out of place," Theresa moaned. As she searched, Theresa *picked* ~~pick~~ up all of her toys and games and put them on the bed. Finally, she *found* ~~find~~ her book under some stuffed animals.

Theresa *looked* ~~look~~ at her bed where she *wanted* ~~want~~ to read her book. She couldn't find a place to sit on the bed.

Page 29

Dear grandma and grandpa

Dates will vary

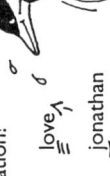

dear grandma and grandpa,

I had a great time visiting you in florida! I liked swimming in the atlantic ocean and jumping in the waves. the shells we found along the beach in daytona were great for my collection. I really liked seeing the dolphins jumping in the water and the pelicans flying overhead. best of all, I liked going to walt disney world! Thanks for a great vacation!

love,
jonathan

Page 30

A Fish Tale

The next time you take out your pole and fill a can with worms to go fishing, think about these questions.

Did you ever hear a dogfish bark? Do angelfish fly? Does a goatfish give milk? Does a catfish drink that milk? Can a parrotfish talk? Can a toadfish hop? Does a butterfly fish like flowers? Can you keep things in a boxfish?

Page 31

What If . . .

What if that little girl really wore blue?
Would little blue riding hood be read to you?
Or what if big Clifford turned out to be small?
Would you enjoy Clifford, the miniature dog?
What if the dwarfs were really quite tall?
Snow White and the Seven Giants might frighten us all.
Last, but not least, is green eggs and ham.
I'm glad they weren't pancakes. Really I am!

Page 32

Seasons

I think of colorful trees and the smell of burning leaves in September, October, and November. These are the gentle months of fall. In the cold, snowy days of December, January, and February, I wear a warm coat, boots, and mittens each day. These are the chilly months of winter. Breezes blow, rain falls, flowers bloom, and birds begin to sing in March, April, and May. These are the exciting months of spring. In June, July, and August, I play ball, go to the park, and run through sprinklers. These are the playful months of summer.

Page 33

Thunder Storm

I lay awake in the quiet house watching the sky grow darker. Suddenly, there was a bright flash of light. There was a loud "crack!" the rain began to splash against my window. I could see the wind bend the tree branches outside. I wanted to hide under my covers, but I knew what I had to do. Trembling, I slipped quickly out of bed. I ran down the hall to the closed door at the end. As I hurried inside, I heard the storm roaring outside. I jumped in the bed. I quickly covered us both with the blanket. I snuggled closer to my sleeping brother so he wouldn't be afraid.

Page 34

Transportation

One day, Mr. and Mrs. Mouse wanted to visit Dr. Mole. Mrs. Mouse's car would not start, so Mr. and Mrs. Mouse jumped on their bicycles. Mr. Mouse's bicycle had a flat tire. Mrs. Mouse called Mr. Rat's Taxi Service, but Mr. Rat's taxi was out of gas.

"We will have to walk," Mrs. Mouse said sadly. "It is a long way."

"I have an idea!" cried Mr. Mouse. "Let's take Dr. Mole's subway. He has dug many tunnels straight to his office."

Page 35

Spring

When Joe woke up, the sun was shining in his window, and he smiled. It would be a fine day to plant his garden. He quickly got up and got out his tractor.

The sun was shining brightly as Joe planted carrots, beans, corn, and beets. He covered the seeds with the warm soil and patted it gently, as if tucking the seeds in bed. Then Joe planted the tomato plants, cabbage, and some turnips, and just as he finished, the sun went away and it began to rain.

Joe smiled. The warm sunshine, the good soil, and the gentle rain would make his garden grow.

Page 36

Starfish

Starfish are not really fish. They live in the ocean. Most starfish ~~has~~ have five ~~armes~~ arms and can grow a new arm if they lose one. The underside of each arm is covered by tube ~~feets~~ feet that help the starfish crawl and get food. The starfish has an eyepot on the tip of each arm that can sense light.
Starfish ~~likes~~ like to eat mussels, ~~clames~~ claws, and oysters. To eat, the starfish ~~pushing~~ pushes its stomach out of its mouth. The stomach ~~surrounded~~ surrounds the food.
Most starfish ~~lives~~ live three to five ~~yeares~~ years, but some may live longer.

Page 37

The Tree House

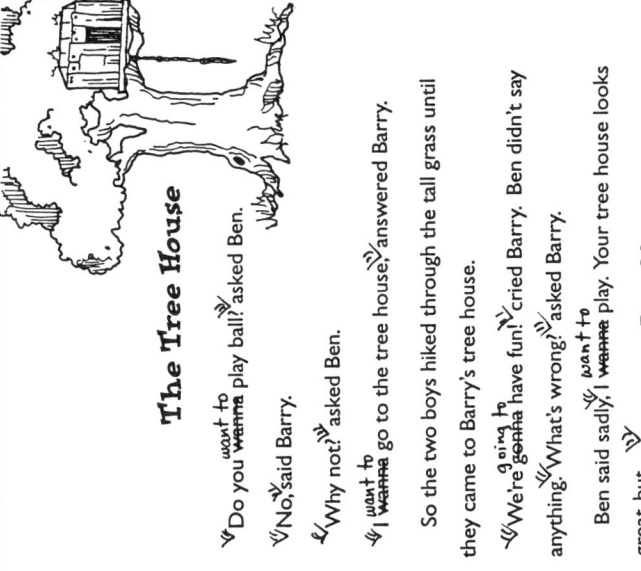

"Do you ~~wanna~~ want to play ball?" asked Ben.

"No," said Barry.

"Why not?" asked Ben.

"I ~~wanna~~ want to go to the tree house," answered Barry.

So the two boys hiked through the tall grass until they came to Barry's tree house.

"We're ~~gonna~~ going to have fun!" cried Barry. Ben didn't say anything. "What's wrong?" asked Barry.

Ben said sadly, "I ~~wanna~~ want to play. Your tree house looks great, but…."

Page 38

"But what?" asked Barry.

"I can't climb that rope, so I can't get in," said Ben.

"~~Doncha~~ Don't you worry, Ben. Just follow me," said Barry. He led Ben to the back of the tree where the branches were low and easy to climb.

"We're ~~gonna~~ going to have fun!" yelled Ben.

Page 39

Soaring

A boy and his father ran across the beach watching Red Kite climb high into the sky. Red Kite was now flying. He wanted to explore. First, He headed for a bird's nest.

"Go home," said the bird in the nest.

"Not yet," said Red Kite. Then, He raced to a telephone pole.

"Go home," said the telephone pole.

"Not yet, I want to fly higher," said Red Kite. Next, He soared toward an airplane.

"Go home," said the airplane.

"Not yet," said Red Kite.

Page 40

"Come down," said the boy.

"Not yet," said Red Kite, jerking on the string.

"Come down," said the boy as he pulled harder.

Finally, Father slowly wound the kite string around the spool.

"I'll come down," said Red Kite as he flew to the ground.

Page 41

Hobbies

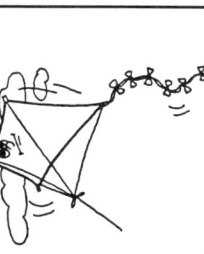

Steve and ~~me~~ I have two favorite ~~hobbys~~ hobbies. One hobby ~~butterflies~~ First, Steve waits for the ~~butterflys~~ butterflies to is catching ~~butterflys~~. Then, land on the ~~daisys~~ daisies and the flower bushes. He passes the net to me, and I scoop up the ~~butterflys~~ butterflies. Next, ~~me~~ I Finally, gently place them in a special insect box. We look through a magnifying glass to observe the ~~butterflys~~ butterflies.

The other hobby Steve and ~~me~~ I have is finding cloud pictures. Some clouds look like trees with ~~cherrys~~ cherries on them. Other clouds look like ~~ponys~~ ponies pulling ~~buggys~~ buggies.

Steve and ~~me~~ I have fun together. Do you have hobbies ~~hobbys~~ that you share with a friend?

Page 42